Foreword

The Dyslexia Institute welcomes the opportunity to update this practical guide for teachers. The first edition, produced in partnership with the Post Office in 1994, has played an important part in our aim to work with schools and help them to meet the needs of over 350,000 dyslexic school-children, many of whom will struggle with the National Curriculum. This new edition takes into account recent developments in theory and practice, and will be of interest to those who have dyslexic pupils, and other literacy strugglers, in their care. It will also be of use to adults with dyslexia, and those working with them in education, training, the community or the workplace.

Since 1972, the Dyslexia Institute has been dedicated to successful learning for children and adults. Institute staff, among others in the field, have continued to develop systems of assessment and teaching which have instilled confidence and unlocked potential. Techniques developed for people with dyslexia can inform the teaching of literacy more widely, and the Dyslexia Institute has welcomed the introduction of many of these techniques into mainstream education through the National Literacy Strategy. Operating nationwide through 26 centres and nearly 150 teaching outposts and in-school units, the Dyslexia Institute offers advice, assessment and teaching, and training programmes for teachers, tutors and teaching assistants.

This book has been developed from the expertise of Dyslexia Institute teachers, teacher-trainers and psychologists, gained in over thirty years of professional practice. The author hopes that all those who use this guide, and other Dyslexia Institute publications, and those who attend our courses, will find them an excellent aid to developing and extending the skills of their students.

Our aim is to ensure successful learning for all.

Janet Townend
Head of Training
The Dyslexia Institute, 2005

NOTE: *For ease of reading I have referred to the dyslexic student as 'he' and the teacher as 'she' throughout. This is the more frequently occurring situation, though, of course, there are many female dyslexic students and male teachers.*

Contents

Introduction

This booklet is an introduction to dyslexia, the difficulties experienced by the dyslexic individual, the assessment process, appropriate teaching procedures, and other ways of dealing with dyslexia. It also touches on the relevance of these procedures to other literacy difficulties and to the wider teaching of literacy.

Note: The term 'specific learning difficulties' is *not* used here as synonymous with 'dyslexia'. The former term covers a range of specific difficulties, of which dyslexia is one. Other specific learning difficulties include dyspraxia, dyscalculia, non-verbal learning deficit, and many others.

Most big skills, such as reading, numeracy or personal organisation, are made up of a number of small sub-skills; it is rather like driving a car. It is necessary to master each of the sub-skills, and then to learn to integrate them into the major skills. The teaching methods that are successful in overcoming dyslexia are the culmination of many years' work; they have grown out of past experience and new insights. How they develop in the future will depend upon increasing our knowledge and expertise.

As teachers, we are not just concerned with teaching people to read, or even to be fully literate, though this is, of course, of crucial importance. We want to develop their skills in all areas of life, to teach the integration of skills and the ability to learn independently, so that our students achieve their potential. The aim of those teaching dyslexic people is the same as the aim of all teachers.

Summary

The aim of a teaching programme is to enable the student to learn:

Skills: literacy, language, memory, mathematics, etc.
Organisation: skill integration, and wider application
Strategies: for independence in learning

The central place of literacy in education, and indeed in society, means that literacy features largely in this book. As you read on, you will discover that our responsibility for our students does not end there.

A literate person is one who can:
- read and write to the level required of his social and intellectual group;
- find meaning in another person's writing and also represent his own thoughts through writing.

To be literate has long been seen as the mark of the educated person. There are three main objectives in teaching literacy:
- learning the structure of language in order to crack the code
- using words accurately for conveying meaning in all modes of communication
- nurturing a real enjoyment and interest in the use of words whether spoken, written or read

The challenge in training teachers is to develop expert craftspeople who can use their tools to produce the best results with the material provided.

The dyslexic student has tried, often very hard, to learn to read, write and spell despite his not possessing the best neurological system for this purpose. In doing so, he may have devised his own faulty strategies for approaching the tasks, which can lead to inaccuracy and bad learning habits. It is vital that he is taught both literacy *and* learning skills.

The penalties for not acquiring the skills of literacy range from social embarrassment to restricted opportunities in education and employment. Secondary penalties are many: poor self-image, lack of confidence in social situations and in the workplace, difficulties in interpersonal relationships and often the development of elaborate strategies to disguise the difficulty from other people.

The specialist teacher must have clear aims for the students, with specific goals related to the age, ability and individual strengths and weaknesses of each one. The skill of literacy encompasses listening, speaking, reading and writing. The dyslexic person may have difficulty in one or all of these areas of literacy attainment, as well as some of the wide range of other problems which are associated with dyslexia and other specific learning difficulties.

For dyslexic people to learn literacy, and other skills, the most effective method has been found to be structured, multisensory teaching. We will look at this in more detail in Chapters 4 and 5.

Targeted teaching
▼
Identifies abilities and difficulties
▼
Prioritises needs
▼
Plans a programme
▼
Teaches only what the student does not already know
▼
Checks that he has learnt what he has been taught
▼
Extends his abilities steadily
▼
Encourages him to set his own goals and standards
▼
Helps him to work against the clock
▼
Successful learning

A good structured, multisensory literacy programme can address individual needs by, first of all:

- Teaching the 'links' between sounds and symbols
- Teaching the 'rules'
- Ensuring that learning is active, not passive

Then building on these basic skills by:

- Practising reading
- Practising writing
- Encouraging a 'thinking' approach
- Nurturing creativity

Then you will unlock the door to literacy.

Despite the heavy emphasis on literacy, the specialist teaching of the dyslexic student must include other vital areas of his learning if he is to succeed and become a fully functioning member of his society. In particular, we must attend to the skills of numeracy, and to the learning, thinking and organisational skills that underpin both literacy and numeracy, and indeed all learning.

Mathematical Skills

- To calculate in school and in later life
- To feel at home in the world of numbers
- To interpret visually presented information
- To understand and judge space and time

Learning and thinking skills

- To develop strategies for learning or accessing information
- To make best use of an inefficient memory
- To train the mind
- To make best use of time
- To develop one's own learning style

CHAPTER 1

Dyslexia: specific difficulties with learning

What is Dyslexia?

Dyslexia causes difficulties in learning to read, write and spell. Short-term memory, mathematics, concentration, personal organisation and sequencing may also be affected.

Dyslexia usually arises from a weakness in the processing of language-based information. Biological in origin, it tends to run in families, but environmental factors also contribute.

Dyslexia can occur at any level of intellectual ability. It is not the result of poor motivation, emotional disturbance, sensory impairment or lack of opportunities, but it may occur alongside any of these.

The effects of dyslexia can be largely overcome by skilled specialist teaching and the use of compensatory strategies.

The Dyslexia Institute, June 2002

In summary, dyslexia is a language-based information processing difficulty. Let us unpack that definition a little. Dyslexic people have difficulties, to varying degrees, in processing, sequencing and retrieving words and other symbols, such as numbers, or musical notation. Inefficiencies in neurological mechanisms give rise to weaknesses in perceiving incoming information through the language centres of the brain. In the early years of life, this can affect the acquisition of spoken language skills, and many dyslexic children enter school with late-developed or still poor spoken language.

Sometimes genetic factors may be involved; scientists have discovered in recent years that features on some chromosomes can be linked to dyslexia. We have known for some years that there is a strong familial link in dyslexia. The figure of four times as many boys as girls being affected is often quoted. Some researchers are now questioning this finding, as more dyslexic girls are being identified. Gender differences in dyslexia are a fairly new area of study, and we will have to wait for more work to be done in this area.

Environment can be influential. For example, a child who has a genetic predisposition to dyslexia, and who suffers from intermittent hearing loss due to repeated ear infections in early childhood may go on to have literacy difficulties. Another child, with a similar history of ear infections, but without the genetic factors, or one in the same family who does not suffer from ear infections, is less likely to display the signs of dyslexia.

However, environmental factors do not *cause* dyslexia; children do not become dyslexic because they have limited opportunities, frequent changes of school, behavioural difficulties, or low ability, though any of these may give rise to literacy learning problems.

Dyslexia does occur among the very bright, the average, and the less academically able population. The popular myth that dyslexic children are usually bright may arise from the fact that it is relatively easy to spot dyslexic difficulties in a child who is otherwise able, and doing well. We sometimes refer to these as the 'puzzling children', because they should be doing better. Similarly, the average child who is underperforming in literacy should be relatively easy to identify, because of the gap between expectation and their attainment in literacy. See Chapter 3 for a discussion of this. The struggling, less able child, may have his or her dyslexia undiagnosed because the difficulties are put down to limited ability. The other group that is hard to identify is made up of very able, or gifted dyslexic individuals, who are doing quite well, so not giving cause for concern. They are often extremely frustrated, prevented from achieving their high academic potential by their literacy limitations.

The first thing that indicates the presence of dyslexia is usually a difficulty in learning to read, write and spell. Of course, dyslexic people will not experience difficulties in all areas, nor will their difficulties be equally severe in all areas. Some dyslexic people will experience severe problems while others will be affected only to a small degree. We will look more closely at the pattern of difficulties later in this chapter.

A brief look at some of the theories of dyslexia

The phonological deficit hypothesis

Since the 1970s the prevailing theories about dyslexia have moved away from 'word-blindness' and links with laterality, towards a deficit in the area of language. This has become increasingly refined into a hypothesis focusing on the phonological, or sound processing, skills. This hypothesis, supported by a great deal of research, is now widely accepted and forms the basis of many successful remedial programmes. The processing and analysis of a string of speech sounds that make up a word appears to be an important prerequisite in the acquisition of literacy; literacy in turn contributes to the development of further phonological skills. These skills are the subject of the next chapter.

A visual processing hypothesis

Within the brain there are two distinct systems concerned with processing visual information; one, the parvocellular system, deals with shape and colour, while the other, the magnocellular system, deals with movement and rapidly changing input. This hypothesis suggests that dyslexic individuals have an impairment of the magnocellular system, leading to difficulties in rapid visual processing. This would impede the reading process. This is believed by some to be the main causal factor in dyslexia. Some work has been done to investigate possible inefficiencies in the rapid processing of auditory information among dyslexic people, and comparisons have been suggested with the visual system. The findings in both areas have been challenged by some other members of the research community.

The cerebellar deficit hypothesis

The cerebellum is a multi-functional part of the brain that deals with, among other things, automaticity and balance. A research team at the University of Sheffield has been working on the hypothesis that a deficit in cerebellar function is at the root of dyslexic difficulties. In order to read, write and spell competently, the learned skills of literacy need to become automatic, and it is suggested that this process is impaired. The researchers have published range of dyslexia screening tools based on this model, including the DST (Dyslexia Screening Test) and versions for adults and young children. One of the subtests assesses an aspect of balance. There is an associated remedial teaching programme, which is not, to date, widely used.

Other theories and models

A number of theories, models and remedial programmes are launched each year, and some of them gain publicity and popularity for a while. The only approach to dyslexia which has been shown to work over time is the educational one, involving high quality teaching. Many specialists in the field agree that the most effective approach is a programme of structured, multisensory teaching, which is discussed in more detail in Chapter 4.

Why do researchers disagree?

People are sometimes puzzled about how researchers so often seem to demonstrate the validity of their own hypothesis, and rarely, if ever, demonstrate the validity of the opposing view. In very simple terms, it is often not what comes out of a piece of research that causes researchers to disagree, but what goes in. In other words, the criticisms may be about such factors as the selection criteria for the subjects of the research (their age, ability, which groups of subjects were not considered eligible, etc.), or how the work was carried out, rather than the results. Different criteria for identifying dyslexia mean that there is variation in the groups of subjects selected for research projects.

Biological factors in dyslexia

Dyslexia tends to run in families. Research into the precise nature of heritability of dyslexia is in its early stages, but more will be known in the next few years. Genetic research has demonstrated, not the presence of a 'dyslexia gene', but dyslexia-related material on at least one chromosome. There are strong indications that dyslexia is genetic in origin.

Since the 1980s neurologists have been examining brains to try to identify differences in the brains of people with dyslexia. At first this was confined to post-mortem examination. The introduction of modern scanning techniques has enabled neurophysiologists to look at the functioning of live brains. Many experiments are carried out in partnership between neurophysiologists and cognitive psychologists, the former recording brain function while the latter set tasks for the subjects to carry out. Again, this research is quite new, but the story so far is that there are noticeable differences in brain activity between dyslexic and non-dyslexic individuals.

How information is processed

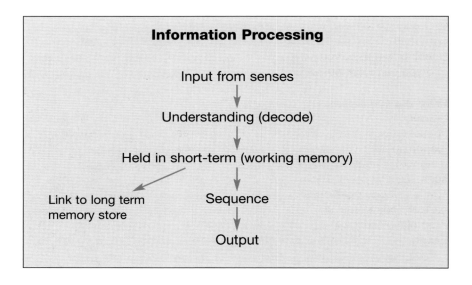

Information Processing

Input from senses

Understanding (decode)

Held in short-term (working memory)

Link to long term memory store

Sequence

Output

Patterns of difficulty

Dyslexia can be positive; a different way of learning and thinking can lead to specific spatial, imaginative, inventive and lateral thinking skills in some people.

A word of warning: dyslexic people are not *automatically* blessed with strong visual-spatial, artistic or creative skills, but some individuals develop very effective compensatory strategies, while others are only able to demonstrate their ability in these areas because they do not involve words.

However, most people with dyslexia will consider it more of a problem than an asset. The most obvious manifestation is a difficulty in learning to read, write and spell, but there may have been warning signs before the child reaches school age. Let us consider some of the other potential problem areas before returning to educational attainment, and literacy attainment in particular.

Perception

Perception is the skill of understanding information received by the senses. This involves isolating the stimulus from others, discriminating between it and other stimuli and relating it to information held in long-term memory. A simple example: if a ringing sound is heard while you are listening to music, you know it is not part of the music, you recognise it, and you can work out whether it is the doorbell or the telephone.

Weak auditory perceptual skills lead to difficulties in discriminating between sounds, hearing sounds in the right order, hearing rhythms in speech; learning through listening will not be easy. Visual perception is responsible for seeing the shapes of words, relative size, judging distances. Other problems may occur in, for example, left to right scanning and other directional skills, or clumsiness due to misjudging space or body position. Many individuals with dyslexia have a specific auditory perceptual skill in the area of phonological awareness. This skill is so closely associated with literacy acquisition that it has been given a chapter of its own in this book.

Spatial and Motor Skills

These two are linked to an extent to each other, and to perception. Spatial awareness difficulties can give rise to poor skills in relative size and shape concepts (puzzles, page layout, size and shape in maths), and to clumsiness (bumping into things, frequent playground collisions, messy eating, etc.). Classroom skills such as copying from the board, and interpreting maps, diagrams and charts may also be affected.

Motor skill difficulties, such as inappropriate pencil grip, also contribute to clumsiness and to poor control of pencil and scissors. Difficulties in hand-eye co-ordination make for problems in catching a ball, in handwriting or in other fine motor tasks such as needlework or construction games. Some pupils may also have trouble with mastery of sports and games, playing a musical instrument (quite apart from the symbol system involved in reading the music), art and craft activities and computer keyboard skills. Difficulties in this area of life and work are particularly discouraging; for the child who struggles with literacy it is very important to identify some strengths, and such skills as sporting ability are highly valued among the peer group. The clumsy dyslexic child seems to be at a double disadvantage.

Of course, many dyslexic individuals are gifted in art and crafts, sports, and on the computer, and some are able musicians. For them, the compensations are important, contributing much-needed self-esteem.

Speech and Language

Poor auditory perception may give rise to the late development of spoken language, including sounds, vocabulary or sentences. Pupils may exhibit poor listening skills, inability to follow verbal instructions, slow response to verbal stimuli, poor comprehension of speech and/or limited expressive language. Word-finding difficulties (that 'tip of the tongue feeling') frequently occur, and sometimes inappropriate use of language (such as failure to understand turn-taking) may be apparent. This should not surprise us; we have identified dyslexia as a language-based difficulty, and many children enter school with a history of late and poor talking, which spills over into late development of literacy, often taking years to catch up. This is linked to phonological skills (see Chapter 2).

Limited vocabulary, particularly in older dyslexic children and adults, may well be a result of a lack of reading experience, by which means much high level vocabulary is normally acquired.

Memory

A difficulty in short-term auditory memory is common to the vast majority of dyslexic people. This impairs the ability to follow instructions, to remember word shapes or names (of people, things or ideas), and to hold information long enough for it to be established in the long-term memory store. As short-term or working memory is a central skill in the learning process, it can be seen that this difficulty will have far-reaching educational consequences.

The precise cause-and-effect relationship is uncertain. Many authorities now suggest that short-term memory competence develops with increasing literacy skill, in which case memory difficulties could not be described as a cause of Specific Learning Difficulties (SpLD). People with memory problems often find it difficult to discard irrelevant or redundant information, which leads to overload and confusion.

Thought Processing

The dyslexic person's thinking may be different from that of his peers; it is likely to be idiosyncratic and may well be inefficient or inappropriate to the purpose. Difficulties may be experienced in linking ideas together, e.g. linking a new concept to existing ones, or generalising, so that a new skill learned in one situation may be applied in others. There may be problems in organising and sequencing ideas, in predicting or extrapolating, with consequent difficulties in essay writing, revision and examinations.

Personal Organisation

In the younger child, difficulties in personal organisation may present as untidiness, forgetfulness (never has his games kit on the right day!) or poor concept of time, days of the week, etc. He may display poor social skills, perhaps responding inappropriately to other children or to adults.

The older student may have great difficulty in organising his time and his work space, in being in the right place at the right time with the right equipment, in storing information tidily (e.g. notes or revision cards) and may frequently find himself in trouble for lateness, failing to hand in work, and so on.

Difficulties of this nature may persist into adult life and dyslexic adults often admit to heavy dependence upon their spouse or secretary to organise their life.

Educational Attainment

The difficulties listed above have serious implications for the learning process, and the dyslexic student is likely to experience a degree of educational failure. This may be severe, affecting his ability to learn to understand print at all, so that he fails to progress in reading and spelling, or he may begin well, and then slow down as he can no longer depend upon a limited sight vocabulary and lacks the skills needed to decode new words. Reading comprehension may be a problem, and he may struggle to find words, sequence ideas and form sentences for written work. The memory and sequencing difficulties along with visuo-spatial weakness could lead to poor progress in maths.

Some very bright dyslexic people, if their difficulties are not severe, may succeed in the education system until they reach the level where pressure of time and higher demands on their organisational skills cause them to begin to fail. This may be at GCSE, at A-level or even in higher education.

Many children, and indeed adults, will experience some degree of difficulty in one or more of these skill areas. This does not mean that they are necessarily dyslexic. However, this list indicates the wide range of difficulties which *may* be experienced by the dyslexic person. A specific learning difficulty, such as dyslexia, may be *suspected* in the student who demonstrates problems in several of the skills listed, which cannot be attributed to other factors such as overall low ability, poor vision or hearing, or emotional and behavioural difficulty.

It is important to remember that emotional problems, factors at home, or low ability, may exist alongside dyslexia; the danger here is to attribute lack of progress to the most obvious factors involved, and miss a specific learning difficulty that could be ameliorated by the right kind of teaching. Equally, it is important to consider the possibility of dyslexia among pupils for whom English is an additional language, if they are failing to make expected levels of progress.

CHAPTER 2

The importance of phonological skills

What are phonological skills?

Phonological skills are the skills of processing speech sounds within language. To be phonologically aware is to be aware of all the individual sounds in a word, and in the correct order. It is easy to see how important this is to reading and spelling: reading, at least at the decoding level, is translating a sequence of shapes on the page to a corresponding string of speech sounds, or phonemes; spelling is the reverse - translating a string of phonemes into a sequence of shapes on the page. If an individual is unable to perceive that string of sounds, then how can he or she convert them into a different symbol system? If you are reading this without difficulty (and I hope you are) it is difficult to imagine how it must be if this skill does not come automatically, where every sound or every letter has to be laboured over.

Some useful definitions

- A **phoneme** is the smallest unit of speech that can change meaning, a single speech sound (so if you change a *p* to an *h* you can change *pen* into *hen*)

- A **syllable** is a beat in a word; every syllable must have a vowel *sound*

- **Rhyme** is the identical sound of the end chunk of two words, irrespective of spelling (*pen / hen, list / missed*)

- **Rime** is the end chunk of a syllable, consisting of the vowel and the following consonant(s), such as the *–en* in *pen* and *hen*. Words or syllables have the same rime when this chunk sounds and **looks** the same, so *-ist* and *–issed* in *list* and *missed* are not rimes

- **Onset** is the initial consonant or consonants in a syllable. Words have the same onset when the beginning **sounds** and **looks** the same, so *cat* and *cup* have the same onset, but *cat* and *city* do not; nor do *city* and *sun*, but *city* and *cycle* do. An onset may have several letters, making one sound, such as *sh* or *th*, or several letters making several sounds, in a blend such as *cl* or *str*

- **Alliteration** is the identical initial sound of two or more words, irrespective of how they are spelled, (*car, kitten, chemist*)

Levels of phonological processing

Phonological awareness can be broken into a series of subskills. Words can be divided into *syllables* (den / tist, o / pen), into *onset* and *rime* (d-en, t-ist, p-en), which also incorporates *rhyming* (den / pen / men, tist / list / twist) and into *phonemes* (d-e-n, p-e-n, t-w-i-s-t). *Segmentation* is the splitting of a word into its components at any level, though it is most often used to refer to splitting into phonemes.

The development of phonological awareness

The early stages of phonological awareness occur as part of normal spoken language development; very small children play with sounds, experiment with rhyme and enjoy sound and rhyming games and stories. Dyslexic children often miss out this early sound play. Many experts believe that the later stages of development, such as segmentation into phonemes, and the perception of stress and intonation patterns, come as a consequence of learning to read. The implications of this are that a dyslexic child may enter school with poorly developed early phonological skills, fail in reading as a consequence, and therefore fail to acquire the higher phonological skills that will support continuing literacy, especially spelling. Vocabulary expansion can also be affected, because we use phonological skills to organise and store new words.

Phonological skills and literacy

Much research has demonstrated the centrality of phonological skills in literacy acquisition. Hatcher, Hulme and Ellis, researching at the University of York, compared the reading progress in four matched groups of children: one group received training in phonological skills only; another had reading experience only; another had a combination of training in phonological skills and reading experience, and the fourth (control) group had no tuition. The results were conclusive: the children who had no tuition made least progress, followed by the 'reading only' group; those who had training in phonological skills did better, but the group that made most progress was the one in which the children received a combination of training in phonological skills and reading experience. This is a powerful argument in favour of the combined approach, but it is also interesting to note that phonological awareness alone was more effective than reading alone.

One US study has shown that for failing readers, just 20 minutes a day, three or four times a week, of training in phonological awareness has huge beneficial effects on literacy development. Other studies have supported these findings. Clearly this is an area which we ignore at our peril.

CHAPTER 3

Assessment

The assessment process

The purpose of assessment is to ascertain whether the student is failing, and to what degree, compared with his peers. If he is behind expected levels, it is necessary to establish whether this is due to: overall low ability; physical factors, such as hearing or sight difficulty; a repeated absence due to illness; emotional or social factors, such as family problems, bereavement, or frequent changes of school; or a specific learning difficulty, such as dyslexia. It is important to remember that more than one factor may be at work in an individual. For example, a failing child who has frequent absences due to asthma attacks may also have a hearing loss or a specific learning difficulty. Differential diagnosis in such cases, as in the case of bilingual children or those speaking English as an additional language, is a delicate and specialised task.

The discrepancy model of assessment

It is necessary, when assessing a student, to ascertain his strengths as well as his weaknesses; these can then be used in teaching. A distinction must be made between his underlying ability (you may call this intelligence, IQ, general conceptual ability, or academic potential) and how he is performing now (i.e. his levels in literacy and numeracy). If there is a discrepancy between these two, the diagnostic assessment of individual skills and a carefully taken case history will, it is hoped, lead to insights into the areas of skill deficit. Some skills, such as phonological awareness, are essential to the development of literacy; other skill deficits may be among the effects of literacy failure. Some aspects of development, such as spoken language, may be useful diagnostic pointers. Other skills considered in diagnostic assessment might include short-term auditory memory and speed of information processing, both frequently occurring in people with dyslexia.

This assessment model is summarised in the diagram below. The diagnostic indicators may help to explain the discrepancy between underlying ability and educational attainment.

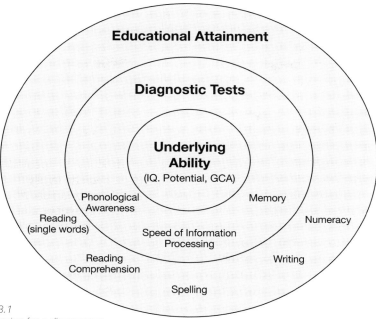

Fig. 3.1
Assessing for a discrepancy

Ideally, detailed assessment at a specialist centre or in school will be carried out by an educational psychologist or a specialist teacher. Some tests are available for non-specialist teachers to use, and although less detailed, they may well be useful as a preliminary to teaching. Wherever a teacher remains concerned, a full assessment should be sought from a chartered educational psychologist. Only an appropriately trained psychologist or specialist teacher is qualified to *diagnose* dyslexia.

Assessing ability

An educational psychologist will normally use either one of the Wechsler battery of IQ tests, (Wechsler Intelligence Scale for Children, 3rd edition or the new (2005) 4th edition, is the most common one) or the British or Differential Ability Scales. Both will yield an overall IQ score and separate IQ scores for verbal and performance (non-verbal) ability, which enables the assessor to compare the subject with his peers. The verbal IQ is recognised as the best predictor of future academic achievement.

These tests are closed to everyone except chartered psychologists; teachers may get some idea of underlying ability by a test of non-verbal and a test of verbal ability. The most reliable aspect of verbal ability to test is vocabulary comprehension. This is the skill which correlates most highly with a full test of ability and is the best single indicator of future academic success. Non-verbal ability may be measured by a test such as Raven's Matrices (pub. NFER Nelson) or the Matrix Analogies Test (a US publication, available from The Psychological Corporation), or the WRAT Expanded Test, (available from The Dyslexia Institute). Two excellent tests of vocabulary comprehension are the British Picture Vocabulary Scale (early childhood to mid-teens), or the similar American Peabody Picture Vocabulary test which covers an age range from early childhood to old age. (Both are available from NFER Nelson.)

Teachers who are qualified in assessment are able to carry out more detailed ability testing, using an instrument such as the WRIT (Wide-Range Intelligence Test), and using an appropriate battery of other measures, to diagnose dyslexia. They will advise about any further assessment, such as speech and language, that may be needed, and an appropriate educational provision. Individuals with a complex pattern of difficulties should be referred directly to an educational psychologist.

Assessing educational attainment

The assessor will look first at reading ability, testing both single word reading and continuous reading. Single word reading tests include SPAR (pub. Hodder); Wide-Range Achievement Test, 3rd edition (known as WRAT-3) (published in the USA and available from the Dyslexia Institute); and the Vernon Single Word Reading Test (pub. Hodder). Continuous reading is often tested using Neale Analysis of Reading Ability (Revised) (pub. NFER Nelson), which assesses accuracy, speed and comprehension of prose passages, up to 13 years. An excellent recent addition to the resources is WRAT Expanded (published in the US and available from the Dyslexia Institute). This includes a reading comprehension test that may be used with students up to 18 years.

Spelling will be assessed in a single word test such as WRAT-3, SPAR, or Vernon, and within a piece of continuous prose writing. Handwriting can also be looked at in continuous writing. Is the size consistent? Is it joined? Are the letters well formed and distinguishable from each other? Writing speed may be assessed by a timed piece of writing, or for a test with age-norms, see the Sentence Completion Test by Robin Hedderly, which may be accessed via the Dyslexia Institute website (**www.dyslexia-inst.org.uk**).

Finally, a number test may be administered. There is a useful one within Differential Ability Scales, but for teachers, the Gilham and Hesse Basic Number Screening Test is a valuable tool, as is the numeracy section of WRAT-3; WRAT Expanded also includes a test of arithmetic.

Typically, the SpLD student will present with an irregular profile of ability, showing areas of strength and areas of weakness, and there will usually be a discrepancy between his *expected* levels of literacy attainment on the basis of the IQ test and his *actual* levels of attainment. Therefore, something is preventing him from achieving his potential.

Diagnostic (skills) testing

Diagnostic or indicative assessment for dyslexia should include a test of short-term auditory memory, a test of phonological skills, and if possible a test of information processing speed. A number of tests are available, but they are best administered by someone who has experience of using such instruments and interpreting the results.

Some of the tests used will be norm-referenced; in other words, the scores will relate to age, either as an age score or as a percentile (the 60th centile means that 40% of the same age will do better, and 60% will do less well). Another way of expressing this information is as a standard score, in which average is 100 (equivalent to the 50th centile). IQ is an example of a test result expressed as a standard score. Two thirds of the population will achieve a standard score between 85 and 115 on an IQ test and any other test standardised to this model.

Other tests are criterion referenced, which means that success or failure is related to the skill. Some skills cannot be graded as an age continuum; a skill such as rhyming is mastered by most children in the pre-school years, but remains a problem to many older dyslexic students. Failure in this skill can be considered diagnostically useful, and the information of criterion-referenced testing is particularly relevant when planning the teaching programme.

A word of warning (several, in fact!)

For the most reliable results, it is essential that modern tests are used where possible, as the norms of older tests are likely to be out of date. Remember that an individual will not perform in exactly the same way on two separate occasions, so test results should not be considered to be 'written in stone'. They are a measure of how one child did on one day with one assessor – tomorrow it may be somewhat different. This is why good tests have 'confidence bands', which indicate the range within which the true score is likely to be. In other words, on one test, if an individual attains a standard score of 95 the true score may lie somewhere between 92 and 98. People being assessed may under-perform, due to internal or external factors, but it is less likely that they would over-perform, so if the same thing is measured twice, the higher score is likely to be nearer to the true score. Having said that, it is striking how high test-on-test reliability can be, in the hands of competent assessors. Assessment is a highly skilled task, and so it is very important that it is carried out by properly trained and experienced people, whether they are teachers or psychologists. Several training providers, including the Dyslexia Institute, offer training in assessment.

Case history

Finally, the importance of information from home and school cannot be overestimated. The parents and teachers who live or work with the child each day will know far more about his strengths and weaknesses in real situations than the tester can discover in an hour or two. The combination of school report, medical and developmental history, home background, other people's appraisal of the problems, and the objective testing will yield a broad picture of the subject's abilities and difficulties, and will help the teacher to plan appropriate teaching.

CHAPTER 4

Principles of teaching

The philosophy behind a structured, multisensory literacy programme

has an organisation	structured and cumulative
uses a technique	multi-sensory
encourages a thinking approach	directed discovery teaching
provides the 'tool kit'	rules and strategies
builds confidence	success
extends abilities	mastery and creativity
gives practice	automaticity
lays foundations	access to the whole curriculum

Literacy is not a single skill; like driving a car, it is a series of little skills, built up into one big skill. For the dyslexic pupil, the acquisition of the big skill has not happened, and he needs to acquire the sub-skills in order to build up literacy.

What else does he need? The dyslexic student needs to be taught organisation of himself and his work, the individual skills of literacy and how to combine them, strategies for successful learning, and he needs to learn to believe in himself.

By the time he reaches the specialist teacher he has already experienced failure; one of the most important tasks of the teacher, therefore, will be to re-build his damaged self-esteem and convince him that he can succeed. The teacher can do this by teaching him in the way in which he can learn, so that his confidence is built by his new experience of success.

'If they can't learn the way we teach, we must teach the way they learn'

Dr H.T. CHASTY - formerly Director of Studies at THE DYSLEXIA INSTITUTE

<blockquote>

Teaching provision must be

- Multisensory
- Structured
- Sequential and cumulative
- Thorough
- Active
- Relevant
- Motivating

</blockquote>

Multisensory teaching

As the name suggests, multisensory techniques are those which use more than one sensory channel for input of information. It has long been agreed that such a method is the most effective way to teach dyslexic students; the stronger channel is used to support the weaker, while the weaker channel is being trained and developed. Material presented in a multisensory way has a better chance of being retained, particularly in view of the poor short-term memory skills of many dyslexic students.

For example, the technique of simultaneous oral spelling is a multisensory one: the student says the word; he then spells it aloud; he then writes it, saying the letters aloud; he then checks it. The sensory input is that he hears and feels himself saying the word, he hears the sequence of letters, he hears them again while feeling his hand write the shapes, he sees the word appear on the page and he can then compare with the original, for a final visual input. How much more effective than just looking at a word and copying it out!

Multisensory techniques are employed to integrate the learning of the sound of a letter, its shape on the written page, and the feel of writing it in cursive script, so that a secure sound-symbol relationship is established for reading and spelling. Students usually find spelling more difficult, and by linking the two, the spelling is 'brought on' by the easier skill of reading the sound.

At all stages, multisensory techniques should be employed for practising reading and spelling, for creative and other continuous writing, for the development of skills such as memory or phonological processing, and later for revision, essay writing and project work.

Multisensory teaching and learning may be applied across the curriculum; it is a technique which would benefit the whole class, not just the dyslexic students.

Structured programmes

The best literacy programmes for dyslexic students follow a carefully developed structure. This means that written language has been broken down into its component parts, which can then be taught, one by one, in a prescribed order. This imposes an organisation and a predictability upon literacy which is very necessary to the student.

The components are not only single letter sounds, but also consonant blends, consonant and vowel digraphs, and the rules of syllable division, suffixing and prefixing.

As a student moves through the programme, the steps taken at each stage are necessarily small, so that there is never a huge amount of new material. He works only with those sounds and rules he has covered, giving him confidence that the materials are within his capability. Each new teaching point stretches him a little, while reinforcing at each stage all that has gone before. This cumulative technique enables the student to assimilate new material at a rate suitable for him; some people will move very rapidly through the programme, while others will go more slowly, spending longer on consolidation at each stage.

Throughout, due to the analytical nature of a structured programme, the student is learning strategies for reading and spelling, by referring to the rules, by breaking down into syllables, by analogy, and by 'sounding-out' blends, digraphs and vowels. This means that he is not dependent on sight vocabulary, which would necessarily be limited by his poor working memory capacity.

Many people are surprised to discover that about 85% of written English is regular and rule-governed. A structured, cumulative literacy programme will give a student access, therefore, to most of what he needs. It is, of course, necessary to teach the useful irregular words, and as the number will be small, multisensory techniques, such as simultaneous oral spelling (see above) will be very effective.

Sequential and cumulative

One important characteristic of a structured programme is that the elements are taught in order. However, if you teach something, then move on, what has been taught can easily be lost as the next thing becomes the focus of attention. The cumulative nature of the teaching is just as important as the sequential. Instead of teaching and practising point 1, then point 2, then point three, a cumulative approach teaches and practises point 1, then teaches point 2, practises points 1 and 2, teaches point 3, practises points 1-3, and so on, so that the body of knowledge *and* skill is being broadened. The advantage of a structured, cumulative programme is the opportunity to keep practising everything which has been learned so far.

Thorough teaching – thorough learning

It is a mistake in the case of the SpLD student to assume that because you, the teacher, have taught him something, he, the student, has learned it. It is too easy to teach, and to move on, leaving the unfortunate student to forget.

An important part of many structured programmes is a series of practice routines, such as using sets of small cards, gradually built up for each student as he works through the programme. These seek to practise, in a multisensory way, sound-symbol associations for reading and for spelling. Irregular words may be practised in the same way. Students practise these routines in their lessons, and on a regular (preferably daily) basis at home, and they become very competent. This competence is extremely important; it means that the associations have become automatic, and automaticity is essential to literacy.

Automatic recall of the sound associated with a symbol (a single letter or a group), or the symbol associated with a sound gives the student access to a strategy for decoding a word in order to read it or spell it. The confidence thus engendered is of immense value, as well as the practical benefit of being able to carry round the strategy in one's head.

We are indebted to an American colleague, Joyce Steeves, for the wise adage:

'Practice makes permanent'

Active learning

Active learning means that the student is involved in what he is doing, and not merely a passive observer of what is going on. For example, when new material is being tackled, the technique of Directed Discovery Teaching is employed; the student is directed by means of questions, tasks, guessing games and so on to discover the new information for himself. He then participates in the recording of the information in a memorable form (such as a letter on a card). He immediately practises it (by reading the sound of the letter) and has opportunities to use it (by reading the sound in words) and to extend the skill (e.g. by learning how to write the letter and spell its sound).

This is a beneficial experience; the pupil remembers because he has done it; it is multisensory and interactive; it is more interesting for him; it encourages him to think, and to develop new strategies for thinking through problems. The student is thus becoming aware of how he learns; this awareness is called metacognition, and is the key to becoming an independent learner. Because of the extra support and help they need, dyslexic students are often inordinately dependent upon their teachers. Because of their experience of failure, they are also frequently discouraged and poorly motivated. Active learning leads to independence through developing metacognition and motivation; this in turn increases success, thus confidence and further motivation follows. It is a virtuous circle. The point at which the teacher and pupil should break into the circle is at active learning.

Relevant teaching

It is a waste of time to teach a student skills which are of no use to him. On the other hand, it is a frustrating experience to teach a student useful, relevant strategies and to watch him fail to make use of them. Relevance, in this context, has two faces.

First of all, the lesson content must be relevant to his age (not too babyish, even if it has to be very basic), to his stage of development (so he can access it readily, but without wasting his time learning what he already knows) and relevant to his strengths and weaknesses. It is pointless to develop his strengths alone, or to concentrate only on what he cannot do. As one student said, 'I go to remedial lessons. The teacher there sees what you can't do and makes you do lots of it.' An awareness of strengths and weaknesses enables the teacher to use the student's strong areas to help the development of the weaker ones.

Materials should also take account of a student's interests; relating to what he is interested in usually has a dramatic effect upon motivation. Finally, the specialist teacher must be aware of the student's current needs within the National Curriculum. This may be well in advance of what he is capable of achieving, and discussion with class and head teachers will be necessary to decide how he may gain access to the curriculum.

ONLY JUST LEARNED CHAINSAW JUGGLING MYSELF..

One of the difficulties which SpLD students experience is in bridging, or generalising what they have been taught to other situations. For example, a child may learn cursive writing, or to divide words into syllables for spelling, and he may be able to do it very well. However, it may never occur to him to transfer either of these skills (or any others) to the classroom, where they would help enormously in his work. Among her many responsibilities, it is for the specialist teacher to point out this relevance, to teach bridging, or skill transfer, and to give plenty of opportunities for practice. She should also, in conjunction with the class teacher, encourage skills to be transferred to the classroom situation. This is perhaps one of the most difficult goals for the specialist teacher and her student to achieve.

Motivation

The list at the beginning of this section says that teaching should be 'motivating'. This is not a special part of the lesson, or even a technique, but something which should happen if all of the other features are in place. Dyslexic pupils have already experienced failure, even the young ones, and they quickly become programmed to expect it. The teacher's confidence in the student's ability to improve has to be relayed implicitly; it is no use just telling them – they will not believe you!

The experience of failure may lead to disaffected behaviour, either active disruption or passivity. The experience of success is usually the best antidote. Motivation usually improves if the student experiences success, and can see the point of what he is being asked to do. One morning, a few years ago, I was writing a lecture on this subject for a Distance Learning course. In the afternoon I was teaching. The mother of my first pupil told me that she was always reluctant to practise her cards because she thought they were babyish. I realised that I had not made sure she understood the purpose of the exercise – it was a bit like the parson who was converted by his own preaching!

Seeing the point of an activity includes finding that it is useful or has relevance in other areas of life, so bridging, or skill generalisation is important. Equally important is having fun! Reading material should be as interesting or amusing as possible, many activities can be turned into games or competitions, and please take account of the student's own interests in finding materials. One of the dullest activities known to man is handwriting practice (well, would you like to do it?). I often get pupils to write out a joke, then they can take it home to tell the family, which makes it slightly more bearable, and gives it a point.

It is striking how many more words some pupils can read or spell in a game or competition than on a worksheet; that should tell us something about the powerful effect of high motivation!

CHAPTER 5

Teaching literacy

The literacy programme

Literacy difficulties are often the first indicators of the presence of dyslexia, or another specific learning difficulty. Failure to learn to read and write soon leads to a sense of inadequacy or poor self-image, and sometimes either disruptive or withdrawn behaviour may follow. Specialist teaching programmes should tackle the learning of literacy in the way in which the student can learn and so aim for early success, a sense of achievement and reversal of the sense of failure. To achieve literacy, a range of skills in reading, writing and spelling have to be mastered.

The skills of literacy

Reading	Writing	Spelling
decoding	cursive handwriting	sound perception
comprehension	practise reading and	sound-symbol
reading experience	spelling skills	association
purposes in	continuous writing	automaticity
reading	purposes in writing	rules of spelling

skill generalisation
The final stage – but it needs to start early
Begin to combine little skills together to make big skills

In the Dyslexia Institute Literacy Programme, as in many other successful programmes, these skills are taught according to the principles outlined in the previous section, namely structured, multi-sensory and cumulative. Individual skills such as phonological awareness, visual discrimination, sequencing and short-term memory form an integral part of the literacy lesson. The emphasis on different skill areas will vary according to the individual strengths, weaknesses and needs of the pupil. Large skill areas such as spoken language, gross or fine motor skills or behaviour will be built into the programme according to need. The assessment findings are very important in planning a teaching programme.

Pace and timing

There are two easy mistakes to make when teaching dyslexic pupils: one is to go too fast, the other is to go too slowly. To go too fast is to lose the opportunity for real learning to take place, with enough reinforcement, so it sticks. To go too slowly will undermine fragile self-esteem, and cause boredom and maybe demotivation or bad behaviour. Keep in mind that dyslexic people tend to be much more able than their literacy skills would suggest.

Making a start in reading

The National Literacy Strategy affords a wonderful opportunity to teach literacy in a multisensory, structured and cumulative way. For example, when introducing a new letter or group of letters, it can be taught for reading (shape recognition, linked to the sound), then for writing (making the shape on paper, and for spelling (linking the sound back to the shape). The new sound can be read and written in words, preferably words that use only the letters already taught.

When the next new letter or letter group is taught, the words used should include the recently taught letters, so there is plenty of opportunity for re-inforcement. For example, if *sh* is taught, followed by *ee*, *sheep* and *sheet* would be good practice words. In this way the sequential programme becomes cumulative and learning becomes more effective. This is not only essential for the dyslexic learner, but good practice across the ability range.

Making progress in reading

Decoding

- Coding is marking text to identify patterns and make it easier to decode. For example:

  - *suffixes or prefixes*
    Underline the base word and box the prefix or suffix, eg.

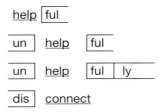

  - *long and short vowels*
    Long vowels make the sound of the letter name, as in *play*, *eat*, *side*, *toe*, *unit* and they are marked with a macron above the vowel (¯) (ā) (ē) (ī) (ō) (ū)
    play eat side toe unit

    Short vowels make the letter sound, as in *pat*, *pet*, *pit*, *pot*, *cut*, and they are marked with a breve above the vowel (ˇ)
    păt pĕt pĭt pŏt cŭt
    (NB *put* has a different vowel sound, so I have not used it as an example).

  - *syllables*
    Words may be divided into syllables, if the syllable division rules have been taught.

Of course, at word level, the skilled task of reading has only just begun, and higher skills must be taught explicitly to the dyslexic learner.

Comprehension

- Answering oral questions
- Answering written questions

- Questions may be
    literal (answers may be found in the text)
    inferential (answers may be deduced or inferred from the text)
    judgmental (readers give their options)
- Cloze procedure is a valuable comprehension activity

To create a cloze exercise, photocopy the page and remove every 7th or 10th word. The student fills in the gaps to make sense (which may not necessarily require an identical word to the one removed). The removed words may be withheld, provided on a folded sheet as a clue or for checking, or listed at the foot of the page, if an easier exercise is required.

Reading for fluency

- **Paired reading**
  Prepare the passage together first, by reviewing any potentially tricky words, coding, or skimming the text (see above). Then the teacher and student read together, in unison. When the student is reading fairly fluently the teacher can 'fade out', but be prepared to join in again when the student hits a difficulty, and keep going with him for a few words, or until he is reading fluently again. If he cannot manage more than a few words without you joining in, the passage is too difficult for this exercise at this stage.

- Student reads onto tape, listens and begins to read in unison with the tape, then sound is turned down and student reads on. Sound is turned up when student finishes reading to see if he has read more quickly the second time.

Saying it out loud

Spoken language has to come before written, and the late or poor talker will be at risk of literacy difficulties. There is space here to mention only two aspects of spoken language which are essential to ongoing literacy acquisition, and which can and must be incorporated into teaching: vocabulary, and phonological awareness. Both need to be worked on in a multisensory way – saying it out loud, hearing and feeling it, and with a visual reinforcement too wherever possible.

Phonological Awareness

Phonological awareness, as we have seen, is central to early literacy development; here are some quick and easy ways of including it in literacy lessons, using what you already have, without any additional time, training or money needed!

- **Syllable Counting**

  Ask pupil to count syllables in some words in the reading book.

  Plastic overlay over the page: pupils ring all two syllable words in one colour, three syllable words in another, etc.

- **Onset-Rime**

  Teacher selects some words (from a page of the reading book) which split easily into onset and rime; pupils split them and think of other onsets for each rime. eg. c at spr at (-*at* is the rime, *c* or *spr* the onset).

- **Alliteration**

  Find all the words on the page which begin with a given sound; think of more words beginning with that sound.

- **Rhyme**

  Teacher selects a word; pupils think of as many rhyming words as possible.

  Teacher selects 3 words, 2 of which rhyme; pupils have to spot the odd one out.

- **Phonemic Segmentation**

  Find all the words on the page which end with a given sound, or have the same vowel sound, or begin or end with the same consonant cluster. Think of some more words with the same feature. (This is harder than the first exercise in this section because you can't always use visual clues.)

Pupil identifies, from oral presentation: initial consonant cluster; final sound (consonant cluster, single consonant or digraph); medial sound (eg *b* in *rabbit*); or vowel sound (stress sound, not name), in a word selected from the reading scheme. For example, the teacher asks:

- What is the final consonant cluster (blend) in ask?
- What is the vowel sound in cake?

Pupils count the sounds (phonemes) in word, without looking, then compare it with the number of letters, to discover that it is not always the same.

A visual aid can help with this task: for younger children, present the caterpillar shape (see below) and some counters. The pupil places a counter on each segment for each sound in the word. The same aid can be used for counting syllables. For older people, place the counters, or some coins, inside the circle and ask them to put one on the line for each sound, or syllable.

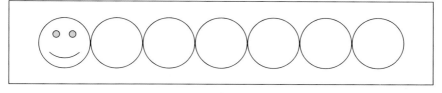

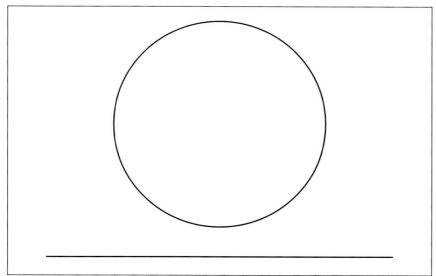

At this point, let me make a plea! *Sounds need to be pure!* Try this exercise:

suh is two sounds, *s* and *uh*; *s* is one sound.

Say these: *suh   muh   puh*
The main thing you hear is the *uh*.

Now say the sound *s* – just as short as you can make it, without the *uh*.

Now say the sound *m* in the same way, and then the sound *p*.
(*s* and *p* should come out as whispers)

Repeat: *s   m   p*
They should sound quite different from each other without the *uh*.

Making sounds like this does two things: it gives the pupils plenty of clues to help them identify the individual sounds, and it replicates the sounds as they are in words. For example, the word *cat* has three sounds: *c a t*, not *cuh a tuh*, which is five sounds (each of those *uh*s is an extra vowel sound!

- A very easily made resource for phonological skills is the 'Sound Card'. The important thing about these cards is that the pupil must say the word and appropriate sound aloud. The exercise requires listening to the sound, not remembering letter patterns, so if the picture clue was a shoe, the target sound would be *sh*, not the initial letter, *s*.

Make card strips like the examples below, with a picture in the space on the left. Clip Art makes this very easy. The pupil identifies the target sound, aloud, writes the word list, then the sentences. A collection of these for different sounds is a useful resource, and of course they can be made much larger for group work.

What blend do you hear at the beginning?

Think of 5 more words with the same blend

Put two of your words into sentences

What sound do you hear at the end?

Think of 5 more words with the same end sound

Put two of your words into sentences

What vowel sound do you hear?

Think of 5 more words with the same vowel sound

Put two of your words into sentences

Vocabulary

Vocabulary is particularly important to higher reading skills, such as comprehension. It can be included as a simple oral activity, linked to reading, conversation, or looking at pictures.

- Teacher asks
  'what does the word …. mean?'
  'what else can the word …. mean?'
  'think of another word for….'

- Teacher asks student to 'find a word that means the same as ….'
  'find a word that is the opposite of …...'
  'find a word that means ……'
  'put the word …. into a sentence of your own'

- Teacher and student look up words in a dictionary and discuss meaning, or use a thesaurus to find alternatives.

Handwriting

A consistent, flowing handwriting style is best; the Dyslexic Institute recommends cursive, which is similar-looking to print, and all letters begin and end on the line (which avoids confusion). Cursive is faster than print, and the smooth flow facilitates better spelling. Teaching cursive from the outset without even teaching print, is strongly recommended.

Writing skills

Writing is usually a dyslexic individual's least favourite activity, and the one that presents most difficulties. One of the keys to improvement is task analysis, or 'eating your elephant in bite-sized pieces'. Any writing task is made up of several elements: ideas, sentence and paragraph structure, handwriting and spelling, grammar, and sequencing.

Planning writing

If it can be planned, by use of a spider-plan or mind-map, to get the main ideas down on paper, they can be ordered numerically in a sensible sequence, then each main point can be developed on the plan. Each main point becomes a paragraph (see below). That will free up the student to concentrate on the grammar, spelling, and so on.

Paragraph structure

- Make up a topic sentence, containing the main point of the paragraph
- Write some supporting sentences (description, argument, evidence, detail, examples, etc.)
- Add a concluding or bridging sentence, to end, or link to the next paragraph

Using reading as a springboard to writing

Student could make up some questions about a passage.
Link with reference skills; encourage students to write up what they already know, or have discovered elsewhere, about this topic.

Six Box Trick		
1. Who?	2. Where?	3. When?
4. What happened first?	5. What happened next?	6. How did it end?

Scaffolding

Writing frames, or a first model paragraph on which to base the others, helps the student to begin to venture his ideas on to paper. The Six Box Trick, above, is an example of a very simple writing frame, and the paragraph structure (above) is a different kind of framework. It should be reproduced using a full sheet of A4 paper.

Spelling

There are two excellent multisensory ways to practise words for spelling:

a) Look-say-cover-write-check, in which the student sees the word first
   - i) Student **looks** at word written down
   - ii) Student **says** word
   - iii) Student says letter **names** in word
   - iv) Student (or teacher) covers word
   - v) Student writes word, **naming each letter as he writes** *(this often-neglected step is actually the key to success)*
   - vi) Student checks word against the original

b) Echo-spell-write-check, in which the student cannot see the word
   - i) Teacher **says** word
   - ii) Student **repeats** word
   continue from iii) above.

For dictation, it is important to structure the activity for maximum success:

   - i) Teacher reads whole sentence
   - ii) Teacher tells student how many parts she is going to split it into
   - iii) Teacher says first part (twice, if you think it necessary)
   - iv) Student repeats aloud (*this is the most important element*)
   - v) Student writes, saying each word aloud as he writes (*also a vital stage*)
   - vi) Student checks spelling of each word against the original and ticks each correct word
   - vii) Spelling errors can be tackled using one of the multisensory methods described above

CHAPTER 6

Dyslexia in the classroom

Support for the teacher

Dealing with the problems of the dyslexic child within a busy classroom is an enormous burden on the class teacher. A teacher may expect to find, on average, one dyslexic student in each class. It is, therefore, essential for teachers to have some guidance on how to cope with meeting disparate needs with limited time and resources. At training courses for teachers the cry frequently goes up, 'How can I help the dyslexic learners while I teach everyone?'

Here are some suggestions for teachers in secondary schools:

- Leave notes up on a board or OHP as long as possible - the dyslexic students take longer to copy

- Tidy board presentation and use of several different colours for different sections will help accurate copying

- Photocopied summary notes help enormously. Hand them out at the beginning, but teach the whole group to annotate, and to highlight or underline key words and themes

- Encourage use of the word-processor for course work, and provide opportunities for keyboard practice

- Mark positively - more ticks for the good bits

- Introduce the teaching of good study skills - this should help all pupils

- Encourage pupils to be aware of and evaluate the strategies they use for study. (This can be done effectively in a study skills programme)

- Provide a list of key vocabulary for your subject, introduce the spelling techniques described in the previous chapter and insist that those words are learned and practised. (Excuse another homework if necessary)

- Well before the exams, get the group to check that they have a complete set of notes. Offer a 'surgery' when they can come to ask you about omissions, or bits they cannot understand, or can't read their own writing!

* Always seek opportunities to praise

Support for the learner

The dyslexic student in the classroom has two main areas of need; survival on a day-to-day basis, and learning. There are a few simple, practical things the class teacher can do to make daily life easier for his SpLD pupil, and others which will enable him to make the most of his learning opportunities in the classroom.

Survival

Organisation
* be patient
* set small tasks (which will build into bigger ones)
* write his homework instructions in a book
* colour code his exercise books (not all red ones)

Behaviour
* have him sitting near you to avoid distraction and to offer discreet help
* praise successes
* try to find something he has done to display
* structure work to ensure some successes
* try to find opportunities to give responsibility

Instructions
* make sure he is attending before you start
* avoid very long instructions
* avoid unduly complex instructions
* list instructions in the order they are to be done (i.e. 'tidy up, then go out', not 'you can go out when you have tidied up'). Read written instructions to him if necessary

Parents
* be aware that parents will be anxious and may appear hostile
* dyslexic children often have a dyslexic parent
* suggest paired reading if appropriate

- ask parents to time homework, to avoid child spending hours on it
- invite them in to help with the class – eg. to hear reading or prepare art materials – not to work with their own children – it could release some of your time

Learning

Literacy

- mark for content if that was the purpose of the exercise
- teach techniques for learning and practising spelling
- encourage the use of the word-processor
- don't make him read aloud in class if he is reluctant
- teach reading and spelling of high frequency and topic-related words
- teach cursive handwriting as early as possible

Topic work

- teach reference skills
- use his artistic gifts
- encourage visualisation before writing, e.g. descriptions
- very poor writers may be able to do 'read and illustrate worksheets'
- slow workers may be able to complete cloze procedure passages
- *Summarising* – in bullet points or using the Six Box Trick (see previous chapter), or by the student writing in his own words
- teach task analysis skills (to the whole class)

Number

- allow concrete help for longer
- a tables square is very helpful, and is not cheating
- a set of small cards with tables on is useful for practice
- supply a card with the sequence of instructions for an arithmetical process
- make sure he understands the language of maths
- make sure he knows where on the page to start, and which direction to go

Groups

- try to have a short time daily with the 'special help' group
- multisensory teaching is best
- develop useful word cards, lists, or personal dictionaries

- allow plenty of opportunities for reinforcement
- work with the special needs teacher

Homework
- make sure he knows what is expected
- ask him to work for a given time, instead of setting a complete task
- give clear, written instructions
- enlist parental support if possible

CHAPTER 7

Confidence – the key to success

Why is it so important?

By the time a student reaches a specialist teacher he has experienced failure, and this will have had a devastating effect upon his confidence and self-esteem; even the pupil who appears outwardly self-assured may have a poor self-image. He will probably have been told at some stage that he is lazy, stupid or never likely to do well. It is the responsibility of the teacher to reverse this if she can do so, to build her pupil's self-esteem by providing the opportunity to experience and practise success.

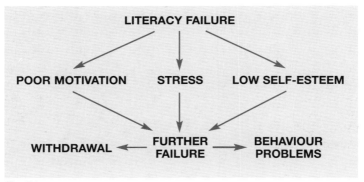

Fig. 7.1

In the dyslexic student, the initial literacy failure is the primary factor in the development of the cycle of failure. Further poor attainment will be exacerbated by low motivation and self-esteem. (Fig 7.1)

The question of where to break into the vicious circle is therefore easy to answer; by attacking the primary cause, and beginning to resolve it, the cycle may begin to be broken down. It is a long, hard, often stressful path to pursue, with setbacks and discouragements, but can in the end be immensely rewarding for teacher and student. This vicious circle can become a virtuous circle. See chapter 4 for a short discussion on increasing motivation in lessons, but remember that success is itself a very powerful motivator.

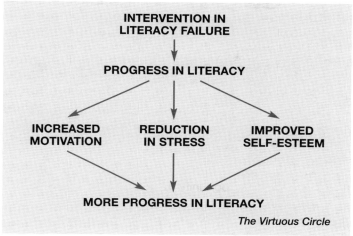

Fig. 7.2

Building for success

Teachers often ask how they can help a dyslexic student in class. Here are a few suggestions; some may seem too obvious to mention and others too difficult to implement. What can be done must depend on the circumstances and on the ingenuity of the individual teacher.

Do
- praise wherever possible
- encourage
- find something that he is good at
- give less homework (e.g. shorter essays, or underline main points to learn)
- mark written work on content (not spelling) – tick what is right instead of crossing what is wrong
- mark on oral responses when possible
- mark according to the criteria covering the purpose of the assignment (so try to ignore the spelling if the purpose is creative writing)
- if reading long words, divide syllables with a pencil line or a small card

- help him to pronounce words correctly
- put him towards the front of the class so you can help discreetly, but avoid making him feel that is some sort of punishment
- make sure he has understood and remembered instructions
- let him work with text book open
- put important words on the board clearly
- give plenty of time to copy from the board – writing on alternate lines in different colours may help
- check whether he knows the alphabet, and that he can say the days of the week and months of the year in the right sequence, and whether he can tell the time
- send an exercise book home with him, with homework assignments written in, and a note of important things to bring tomorrow, e.g. swimming things
- have expectation of success

Don't
- make a dyslexic student read aloud in public if reluctant
- ridicule or employ sarcasm
- correct *all* mistakes in written work – it's too discouraging (see marking guidelines earlier in this chapter)
- give lists of spelling words to learn; two or three are as many as he will manage, and it is better if they are related, eg. plate, cake, name
- make him write out work again
- compare him with others
- make him change his writing (put loops if he doesn't, for example); but see handwriting advice in Chapter 5

Remember
An individual with dyslexia:
- tires more quickly than a non-dyslexic person; far greater concentration is required
- may read a passage correctly yet not get the sense of it
- may have great difficulty with figures (e.g. learning tables), reading music or anything which entails interpreting symbols
- usually has difficulty learning foreign languages
- is inconsistent in performance
- may omit a word or words, or write one twice
- suffers from constant nagging uncertainty
- cannot take good notes because he cannot listen and write at the same time

- may have great difficulty in finding his place again when he looks away from a book he is reading, or a board he is copying from
- reads slowly because of his difficulties, so is always under pressure of time
- will probably be personally disorganised – he may also be clumsy and forgetful, no matter how hard he tries
- is likely to have difficulty following a string of instructions.

CHAPTER 8

Dyslexia beyond school age

On being a dyslexic adult

Much of what has gone before applies as well to those over the age of compulsory education as to those still in the midst of it. While it is true that many dyslexic adults begin to flourish once they are free of the necessity to learn literacy, for the majority, the lack of skills continues to be a source of stress and even shame. They have been subjected to the vicious circle described in the previous chapter.

This lack of skills can range from a difficulty in understanding complex text, and in producing high-level written work, to little or no reading and writing at all. Some adults try literacy classes at their local college, only to find that the class is too large, the pace too fast, or the work beyond their levels of skill and confidence. They feel uncomfortable, and they drop out of the class.

Others only discover the real problem when their children are diagnosed dyslexic; many dyslexic parents begin to recognise their difficulties in their children, and the diagnosis leads them to seek assessment, or to self-assess, informally. The discovery that one is not, after all, 'thick' can be life-changing.

However, it is the case that too many people are still leaving school lacking an appropriate level of basic skills, and many adults are carrying round a secret burden. Many will be very reluctant to seek help, and especially reluctant to make themselves vulnerable by being assessed.

What are the differences between dyslexic children and dyslexic adults?

- Adults have often used their intelligence to develop sophisticated coping strategies
- Adults have usually had opportunities to find work that suits their strengths

- Adults have had to live with the difficulties for longer, and may have even more fragile self-esteem than the younger people
- Older adults will have been to school before dyslexia was well-recognised, and may have no idea what the nature of their difficulty is

There are far, far more similarities, however. Adults with dyslexia have the same underlying difficulties in information processing, short-term auditory memory and phonological awareness as children with dyslexia. They have the same need for structured, multisensory teaching if they are to succeed in improving their literacy skills.

Particular learning needs of adults

In addition to tuition to improve the skills of reading, writing and spelling, adults with dyslexia may seek help and support in other areas:

- Form-filling
- Banking, voting, employment and tax issues
- Shopping
- Workplace issues
- Information gathering
- Practical numeracy, including finances
- Travel, timetables, etc
- Parenting their own children

The list could go on.

The role of the tutor

Counsellor

Even more than with a young person, the tutor of an adult with dyslexia needs to be a friend and supporter. Perhaps the most valuable skill is that of listening. Most tutors are not trained as counsellors, but need to know enough of counselling skills to be able to listen carefully and non-judgmentally, offering the client *unconditional positive regard*. Questions, gently put, should be open, inviting the client to expand, not closed, requiring only a one-word answer.

Above all, as a tutor, try not to give a great deal of advice; on the other hand, seek, by asking questions, to help the client to work out the solutions to his or her own problems. It is not respecting of another person to assume that the tutor role makes one a better judge of his personal circumstances than the person himself. Advice should ideally be confined to situations in which the tutor's professional input is necessary.

Example:

Client: I am being picked on at work (gives details). What do you think I should do?

Tutor: What are your options?

But not: Well, you must go to your line manager, or......

The working partnership

An adult student will come for tuition with some idea of what he or she wants and needs from the lessons. This might be very realistic, or cautious and conservative, or wildly ambitious. Following assessment, the tutor will have some idea of the client's strengths and difficulties, and literacy levels.

Planning the teaching programme will be a negotiation between the two of them, matching up as far as possible the student's aspirations with what the tutor has to offer. The tutor's skill at this stage is in helping the client to understand that some of his difficulties are due to his existing literacy skills being built on shaky foundations. For example, a student who has trouble with spelling vowel sounds needs not (as he may be expecting) to learn spelling, but to deal with underlying difficulties in phonological perception. It may be necessary to appear to be going back before going forward. This can be acceptable to the student who understands why, and who feels valued by, and confident in his tutor. This relationship is central to making progress.

The tutor will engage the student as a full partner in developing a programme. A partner relationship ensures that the student understands the nature of the difficulty, what will help and why, and the purpose of the work being done. Evaluation can be a mutual activity, with the student helped to recognise and celebrate progress. However, too fulsome praise can be equally patronising, and reduce feelings of self-worth. '*If getting this infantile stuff right is an achievement, I must be really stupid*'.

The tutor will need to be very careful to reassure the student that the work is not childish or insulting. For example, the vocabulary used should always be age-appropriate, and if alphabet sequencing has to be taught, avoid children's wooden letters. Even readily decodable text can be adult in content:

> *The dentist's assistant has long legs.*

is as easily decoded as

> *Ben did a handstand in the sandpit.*

Summary

An important key to success in teaching adults is the relationship between tutor and student (or group of students). Even group work has to take account of individual differences in the level of skill and the nature of the difficulty.

Teaching for adults has to be structured, multisensory, and very importantly, useful. Humour, support, and being listened to will make the experience a positive one.

The principles of usefulness and partnership described above can equally well be applied to the teaching of younger people, including children.

Useful names and addresses

Publishers

Ann Arbor Publishers
P0 Box 1, Balford, Northumberland NE7O 7JX

Barrington Stoke (books for dyslexic readers)
10 Belford Terrace, Edinburgh, EH4 3DQ (Tel. 0131 315 4933)

Cambridge University Press
The Pitt Building, Trumpington Street, Cambridge CB2 1RP

The Dyslexia Institute
Park House, Wick Road, Egham, Surrey, TW20 0HH
(Tel. 01784 222300)

Harcourt Assessment (formerly The Psychological Corporation)
Halley Court, Jordan Hill, Oxford OX2 8EJ

Learning Development Aids
Duke Street, Wisbech, Cambs PEl3 2AE

Learning Materials Ltd.
Dixon Street, Wolverhampton WV2 2BX

SRA
Newtown Road, Henley on Thames, Oxon RG9 1 EW

Schofield & Sims Ltd.
Dogley Mill, Fenay Bridge, Huddersfield, Yorks

Taskmaster Ltd.
Morris Road, Leicester LE2 6BR

Other useful addresses

British Dyslexia Association
98 London Road, Reading, Berks RG1 5AU
for contact with local Dyslexia Associations and a variety of
publications,leaflets and conferences.

DI Trading Ltd
Park House, Wick Road, Egham, Surrey TW20 0HH
(Tel. 01784 222300 / Fax. 01784 222333 / www.dyslexia-inst.org.uk)

BetterBooks
3, Paganel Drive, Dudley, West Midlands DY1 4AZ
for a wide range of SEN books and book-based teaching resources,
with a large dyslexia section.

SEN Marketing Ltd
618 Leeds Road, Outwood, Wakefield, WF1 2LT
(Tel/Fax. 01924 871697)
for a wide range of SEN books and book-based teaching resources,
with a large dyslexia section.

Reading Reading Centre
Reading Language Information Centre, University of Reading,
Bulmershe Court, Earley, Reading, Berks. RG6 HY

The Royal College of Speech and Language Therapists
5 Bath Place, Rivington Street, London EC1

The Dyslexia Institute as a resource

The Dyslexia Institute, founded in 1972, is dedicated to successful learning for dyslexic people. It has grown to be a national organisation with 26 centres and nearly 150 outposts and in-school units. The Training Service reaches teachers across the UK and on five continents by live and Distance Learning courses.

The Institute offers assessment, specialist teaching, including units within schools, adult classes, teacher training (from post-graduate level to one-day awareness courses), INSET days in schools, publications (books, teaching materials and leaflets), membership of its professional association, The Dyslexia Institute Guild, and exhibitions. For details of any of these services please contact:

> **The Information Officer**
> **The Dyslexia Institute**
> **Park House**
> **Wick Road**
> **Egham**
> **Surrey**
> **TW20 0HH**
> **Telephone 01784 222300**
> **e-mail information@dyslexia-inst.org.uk**
> **or visit www.dyslexia-inst.org.uk**

Details of courses for teachers and teaching assistants may be found on the website, or by contacting the **National Training Office** at the above address, Telephone **01784 222304** or e-mail **training@dyslexia-inst.org.uk**

For a catalogue of books and teaching resources, or to place an order, contact **DI Trading** (at the above address), Telephone **01784 222339** or e-mail **trading@dyslexia-inst.org.uk**